Super Handy P|

Phone Number En

Calendar Da

Weekly Planner

Bonuses

Website Passwords Log

Personal Goals

Vacation Planning

Packing List

Party Planning

Christmas Day Planner

Grocery List

Notebook

Lined Pages

Notes

Grid Dots

Gift ideas with a personal touch

CustomNameGifts.com

Follow Us On Instagram

@MariaLeonaDesign

Important Info

FAMILY NAME:

ADDRESS:

HOME PHONE:

IN AN EMERGENCY CALL:

PARENT 1

NAME:

WORK PHONE:

CELL PHONE:

PARENT 2

NAME:

WORK PHONE:

CELL PHONE:

CHILDREN'S NAMES

CHILDREN'S CELL PHONE NUMBERS

SCHOOL NAME(S)

SCHOOL PHONE NUMBERS

EXTENDED FAMILY

NEIGHBORS & FRIENDS

NOTES:

Phone Numbers - eMails

MILY

FRIENDS

EQUENT PLAYDATES

NEIGHBORS

BYSITTERS

SCHOOLS/DAYCARE

OS' AFTER-SCHOOL PROGRAMS

KIDS' FAVORITE ATTRACTIONS

LONS

GYMS/CLUBS

TAURANTS

TAKE-OUT/DELIVERY

r

GROOMER

Phone Numbers - eMails

CONTRACTORS

HANDYMAN

REPAIRS

CLEANING SERVICES

LAWN SERVICE

SNOW REMOVAL

GARBAGE PICKUP

RECYCLING PICKUP

DECORATOR

OTHER

NOTES:

Phone Numbers - eMails

NTRACTORS

HANDYMAN

AIRS

CLEANING SERVICES

/N SERVICE

SNOW REMOVAL

BAGE PICKUP

RECYCLING PICKUP

CORATOR

OTHER

OTES:

January

Monthly Focus

1 _____
2 _____
3 _____

Special Dates

_____ _____
_____ _____
_____ _____
_____ _____
_____ _____

Home Keeping Tasks

☐ _____
☐ _____
☐ _____
☐ _____
☐ _____
☐ _____
☐ _____

Goals for the Month

_____ ☐
_____ ☐
_____ ☐
_____ ☐
_____ ☐
_____ ☐

_____ ☐
_____ ☐
_____ ☐
_____ ☐
_____ ☐
_____ ☐

_____ ☐
_____ ☐
_____ ☐
_____ ☐
_____ ☐
_____ ☐

Notes

February

onthly Focus

Top Three Things

1 _____
2 _____
3 _____

Home Keeping Tasks

- ☐ _____
- ☐ _____
- ☐ _____
- ☐ _____
- ☐ _____
- ☐ _____
- ☐ _____

als for the Month

- ☐ _____
- ☐ _____
- ☐ _____
- ☐ _____
- ☐ _____
- ☐ _____

Notes

- ☐ _____
- ☐ _____
- ☐ _____
- ☐ _____
- ☐ _____
- ☐ _____

- ☐ _____
- ☐ _____
- ☐ _____
- ☐ _____
- ☐ _____
- ☐ _____

March

Monthly Focus

1 _____
2 _____
3 _____

Special Dates

_____ _____
_____ _____
_____ _____
_____ _____
_____ _____

Home Keeping Tasks

☐ _____
☐ _____
☐ _____
☐ _____
☐ _____
☐ _____
☐ _____

Goals for the Month

_____ ☐
_____ ☐
_____ ☐
_____ ☐
_____ ☐
_____ ☐

_____ ☐
_____ ☐
_____ ☐
_____ ☐
_____ ☐
_____ ☐

_____ ☐
_____ ☐
_____ ☐
_____ ☐
_____ ☐
_____ ☐

Notes

April

Monthly Focus

1 _____
2 _____
3 _____

Special Dates

___ _____
___ _____
___ _____
___ _____
___ _____

Home Keeping Tasks

☐ _____
☐ _____
☐ _____
☐ _____
☐ _____
☐ _____
☐ _____

Goals for the Month

☐ _____
☐ _____
☐ _____
☐ _____
☐ _____
☐ _____

☐ _____
☐ _____
☐ _____
☐ _____
☐ _____
☐ _____

☐ _____
☐ _____
☐ _____
☐ _____
☐ _____
☐ _____

Notes
_____
_____
_____
_____
_____
_____
_____
_____
_____
_____
_____
_____
_____
_____
_____
_____
_____
_____
_____
_____
_____
_____
_____

May

Monthly Focus

1 _____
2 _____
3 _____

Special Dates

____ _____
____ _____
____ _____
____ _____
____ _____

Home Keeping Tasks

☐ _____
☐ _____
☐ _____
☐ _____
☐ _____
☐ _____
☐ _____

Goals for the Month

_____ ☐
_____ ☐
_____ ☐
_____ ☐
_____ ☐
_____ ☐

_____ ☐
_____ ☐
_____ ☐
_____ ☐
_____ ☐
_____ ☐

_____ ☐
_____ ☐
_____ ☐
_____ ☐
_____ ☐
_____ ☐

Notes

_____
_____
_____
_____
_____
_____
_____
_____
_____
_____
_____
_____
_____
_____
_____
_____
_____
_____
_____

June

Top Three Things

1 _____
2 _____
3 _____

Special Dates

___ _____
___ _____
___ _____
___ _____
___ _____

Home Keeping Tasks

☐ _____
☐ _____
☐ _____
☐ _____
☐ _____
☐ _____
☐ _____

Is for the Month

_____ ☐
_____ ☐
_____ ☐
_____ ☐
_____ ☐
_____ ☐

_____ ☐
_____ ☐
_____ ☐
_____ ☐
_____ ☐
_____ ☐

_____ ☐
_____ ☐
_____ ☐
_____ ☐
_____ ☐
_____ ☐

Notes

_____
_____
_____
_____
_____
_____
_____
_____
_____
_____
_____
_____
_____
_____
_____
_____
_____
_____
_____
_____
_____
_____
_____
_____
_____

July

Monthly Focus

Top Three Things

1 _____
2 _____
3 _____

Special Dates

_____ _____
_____ _____
_____ _____
_____ _____
_____ _____

Home Keeping Tasks

☐ _____
☐ _____
☐ _____
☐ _____
☐ _____
☐ _____
☐ _____

Goals for the Month

☐ _____
☐ _____
☐ _____
☐ _____
☐ _____
☐ _____

☐ _____
☐ _____
☐ _____
☐ _____
☐ _____
☐ _____

☐ _____
☐ _____
☐ _____
☐ _____
☐ _____
☐ _____

Notes

_____
_____
_____
_____
_____
_____
_____
_____
_____
_____
_____
_____
_____
_____
_____
_____
_____
_____
_____
_____
_____
_____
_____
_____
_____

August

onthly Focus

als for the Month

Top Three Things

1 _____
2 _____
3 _____

Home Keeping Tasks

☐ _____
☐ _____
☐ _____
☐ _____
☐ _____
☐ _____
☐ _____

Notes

September

Monthly Focus

1 _____
2 _____
3 _____

Special Dates

_____ _____
_____ _____
_____ _____
_____ _____
_____ _____

Home Keeping Tasks

☐ _____
☐ _____
☐ _____
☐ _____
☐ _____
☐ _____
☐ _____

Goals for the Month

_____ ☐
_____ ☐
_____ ☐
_____ ☐
_____ ☐
_____ ☐

_____ ☐
_____ ☐
_____ ☐
_____ ☐
_____ ☐
_____ ☐

_____ ☐
_____ ☐
_____ ☐
_____ ☐
_____ ☐
_____ ☐

Notes

_____
_____
_____
_____
_____
_____
_____
_____
_____
_____
_____
_____
_____
_____
_____
_____
_____
_____
_____
_____

October

Top Three Things

1 _____
2 _____
3 _____

Special Dates

_____
_____
_____
_____
_____

Home Keeping Tasks

☐ _____
☐ _____
☐ _____
☐ _____
☐ _____
☐ _____
☐ _____

als for the Month

_____ ☐
_____ ☐
_____ ☐
_____ ☐
_____ ☐
_____ ☐

_____ ☐
_____ ☐
_____ ☐
_____ ☐
_____ ☐
_____ ☐

_____ ☐
_____ ☐
_____ ☐
_____ ☐
_____ ☐
_____ ☐

Notes

_____
_____
_____
_____
_____
_____
_____
_____
_____
_____
_____
_____
_____
_____
_____
_____
_____
_____
_____
_____
_____

November

Monthly Focus

1 _____
2 _____
3 _____

Special Dates

_____ _____
_____ _____
_____ _____
_____ _____
_____ _____

Home Keeping Tasks

☐ _____
☐ _____
☐ _____
☐ _____
☐ _____
☐ _____
☐ _____

Goals for the Month

_____ ☐
_____ ☐
_____ ☐
_____ ☐
_____ ☐
_____ ☐

_____ ☐
_____ ☐
_____ ☐
_____ ☐
_____ ☐
_____ ☐

_____ ☐
_____ ☐
_____ ☐
_____ ☐
_____ ☐
_____ ☐

Notes

December

athly Focus

Top Three Things

1 _____
2 _____
3 _____

Special Dates

— _____
— _____
— _____
— _____
— _____

Home Keeping Tasks

☐ _____
☐ _____
☐ _____
☐ _____
☐ _____
☐ _____
☐ _____

s for the Month

☐
☐
☐
☐
☐
☐

☐
☐
☐
☐
☐
☐

☐
☐
☐
☐
☐
☐

Notes

_____
_____
_____
_____
_____
_____
_____
_____
_____
_____
_____
_____
_____
_____
_____
_____
_____
_____
_____
_____
_____
_____
_____

Week 1

Monday

Tuesday

Wednesday

Thursday

Friday

Saturday

Sunday

Places to Go

- ○
- ○
- ○
- ○
- ○
- ○

People to See

- ○
- ○
- ○
- ○
- ○
- ○

Things to Do

- ○
- ○
- ○
- ○
- ○
- ○
- ○
- ○
- ○
- ○
- ○
- ○
- ○

Special Reminders

- ○
- ○
- ○
- ○
- ○
- ○

Week 2

onday

iesday

ednesday

iursday

iday

turday

nday

Places to Go

People to See

Things to Do

Special Reminders

Week 3

Monday

Tuesday

Wednesday

Thursday

Friday

Saturday

Sunday

Places to Go

People to See

Things to Do

Special Reminders

Week 4

Monday

Tuesday

Wednesday

Thursday

Friday

Saturday

Sunday

Places to Go
- ○
- ○
- ○
- ○
- ○
- ○

People to See
- ○
- ○
- ○
- ○
- ○
- ○

Things to Do
- ○
- ○
- ○
- ○
- ○
- ○
- ○
- ○
- ○
- ○
- ○
- ○

Special Reminders
- ○
- ○
- ○
- ○
- ○
- ○

Week 5

Monday

Tuesday

Wednesday

Thursday

Friday

Saturday

Sunday

Places to Go

People to See

Things to Do

Special Reminders

Week 6

nday

sday

dnesday

rsday

ay

urday

day

Places to Go
○
○
○
○
○
○

People to See
○
○
○
○
○
○

Things to Do
○
○
○
○
○
○
○
○
○
○
○
○

Special Reminders
○
○
○
○
○
○
○

Week 7

Monday

Tuesday

Wednesday

Thursday

Friday

Saturday

Sunday

Places to Go

People to See

Things to Do

Special Reminders

Week 8

onday

esday

ednesday

ursday

day

turday

nday

Places to Go

○
○
○
○
○
○

People to See

○
○
○
○
○

Things to Do

○
○
○
○
○
○
○
○
○
○
○
○

Special Reminders

○
○
○
○
○
○
○

Week 8

Monday

Tuesday

Wednesday

Thursday

Friday

Saturday

Sunday

Places to Go

People to See

Things to Do

Special Reminders

Week 9

onday

esday

ednesday

ursday

day

turday

nday

Places to Go

- ○
- ○
- ○
- ○
- ○
- ○

People to See

- ○
- ○
- ○
- ○
- ○
- ○

Things to Do

- ○
- ○
- ○
- ○
- ○
- ○
- ○
- ○
- ○
- ○
- ○

Special Reminders

- ○
- ○
- ○
- ○
- ○
- ○

Week 10

Monday

Tuesday

Wednesday

Thursday

Friday

Saturday

Sunday

Places to Go
-
-
-
-
-
-

People to See
-
-
-
-
-
-

Things to Do
-
-
-
-
-
-
-
-
-
-
-
-

Special Reminders
-
-
-
-
-
-

Week 11

day

sday

Inesday

rsday

ay

urday

day

Week 12

Monday

Tuesday

Wednesday

Thursday

Friday

Saturday

Sunday

Places to Go

People to See

Things to Do

Special Reminders

Week 13

onday

esday

ednesday

ursday

day

turday

nday

Places to Go

○
○
○
○
○
○

People to See

○
○
○
○
○
○

Things to Do

○
○
○
○
○
○
○
○
○
○
○
○

Special Reminders

○
○
○
○
○
○
○

Week 14

Monday

Tuesday

Wednesday

Thursday

Friday

Saturday

Sunday

Places to Go

People to See

Things to Do

Special Reminders

Week 15

nday

esday

dnesday

ırsday

day

urday

ıday

Places to Go

- ○
- ○
- ○
- ○
- ○
- ○

People to See

- ○
- ○
- ○
- ○
- ○
- ○

Things to Do

- ○
- ○
- ○
- ○
- ○
- ○
- ○
- ○
- ○
- ○
- ○
- ○

Special Reminders

- ○
- ○
- ○
- ○
- ○
- ○
- ○

Week 16

Monday

Tuesday

Wednesday

Thursday

Friday

Saturday

Sunday

Places to Go

- ○
- ○
- ○
- ○
- ○
- ○

People to See

- ○
- ○
- ○
- ○
- ○
- ○

Things to Do

- ○
- ○
- ○
- ○
- ○
- ○
- ○
- ○
- ○
- ○
- ○
- ○

Special Reminders

- ○
- ○
- ○
- ○
- ○
- ○

Week 17

nday

sday

dnesday

rsday

ay

urday

day

Places to Go
- ○
- ○
- ○
- ○
- ○
- ○

People to See
- ○
- ○
- ○
- ○
- ○
- ○

Things to Do
- ○
- ○
- ○
- ○
- ○
- ○
- ○
- ○
- ○
- ○
- ○
- ○

Special Reminders
- ○
- ○
- ○
- ○
- ○
- ○
- ○

Week 18

Monday

Tuesday

Wednesday

Thursday

Friday

Saturday

Sunday

Places to Go

- ○
- ○
- ○
- ○
- ○
- ○

People to See

- ○
- ○
- ○
- ○
- ○
- ○

Things to Do

- ○
- ○
- ○
- ○
- ○
- ○
- ○
- ○
- ○
- ○
- ○
- ○

Special Reminders

- ○
- ○
- ○
- ○
- ○
- ○

Week 19

onday

esday

ednesday

ursday

day

turday

nday

- ○
- ○
- ○
- ○
- ○
- ○

People to See

- ○
- ○
- ○
- ○
- ○
- ○

Things to Do

- ○
- ○
- ○
- ○
- ○
- ○
- ○
- ○
- ○
- ○
- ○
- ○

Special Reminders

- ○
- ○
- ○
- ○
- ○
- ○

Week 20

Monday

Tuesday

Wednesday

Thursday

Friday

Saturday

Sunday

Places to Go

People to See

Things to Do

Special Reminders

Week 21

nday

sday

dnesday

rsday

lay

urday

day

Places to Go

- ○
- ○
- ○
- ○
- ○
- ○

People to See

- ○
- ○
- ○
- ○
- ○
- ○

Things to Do

- ○
- ○
- ○
- ○
- ○
- ○
- ○
- ○
- ○
- ○
- ○

Special Reminders

- ○
- ○
- ○
- ○
- ○
- ○

Week 22

Monday

Tuesday

Wednesday

Thursday

Friday

Saturday

Sunday

Places to Go

People to See

Things to Do

Special Reminders

Week 23

day

sday

nesday

rsday

ay

rday

day

○
○
○
○
○
○

People to See

○
○
○
○
○
○

Things to Do

○
○
○
○
○
○
○
○
○
○
○
○

Special Reminders

○
○
○
○
○
○
○

Week 24

Monday

Tuesday

Wednesday

Thursday

Friday

Saturday

Sunday

Places to Go

-
-
-
-
-
-

People to See

-
-
-
-
-
-

Things to Do

-
-
-
-
-
-
-
-
-
-
-
-

Special Reminders

-
-
-
-
-
-
-

Week 25

nday

esday

ednesday

ursday

day

urday

nday

Places to Go

- ◯
- ◯
- ◯
- ◯
- ◯
- ◯

People to See

- ◯
- ◯
- ◯
- ◯
- ◯

Things to Do

- ◯
- ◯
- ◯
- ◯
- ◯
- ◯
- ◯
- ◯
- ◯
- ◯
- ◯

Special Reminders

- ◯
- ◯
- ◯
- ◯
- ◯
- ◯
- ◯

Week 26

Monday

Tuesday

Wednesday

Thursday

Friday

Saturday

Sunday

Places to Go

- ○
- ○
- ○
- ○
- ○
- ○

People to See

- ○
- ○
- ○
- ○
- ○

Things to Do

- ○
- ○
- ○
- ○
- ○
- ○
- ○
- ○
- ○
- ○
- ○

Special Reminders

- ○
- ○
- ○
- ○
- ○
- ○

Week 27

onday

esday

ednesday

ursday

day

turday

nday

Places to Go

○
○
○
○
○
○

People to See

○
○
○
○
○
○

Things to Do

○
○
○
○
○
○
○
○
○
○
○
○

Special Reminders

○
○
○
○
○
○

Week 28

Monday

Tuesday

Wednesday

Thursday

Friday

Saturday

Sunday

People to See

Things to Do

Special Reminders

Week 29

day

day

nesday

sday

ay

rday

lay

Places to Go

○
○
○
○
○
○

People to See

○
○
○
○
○
○

Things to Do

○
○
○
○
○
○
○
○
○
○
○
○

Special Reminders

○
○
○
○
○
○
○

Week 30

Monday

Tuesday

Wednesday

Thursday

Friday

Saturday

Sunday

Places to Go

- ○
- ○
- ○
- ○
- ○
- ○

People to See

- ○
- ○
- ○
- ○
- ○
- ○

Things to Do

- ○
- ○
- ○
- ○
- ○
- ○
- ○
- ○
- ○
- ○
- ○
- ○

Special Reminders

- ○
- ○
- ○
- ○
- ○
- ○

Week 31

nday

esday

dnesday

ursday

day

urday

1day

Places to Go

People to See

Things to Do

Special Reminders

Week 32

Monday

Tuesday

Wednesday

Thursday

Friday

Saturday

Sunday

Places to Go

People to See

Things to Do

Special Reminders

Week 33

nday

esday

dnesday

ırsday

lay

urday

ıday

Week 34

Monday

Tuesday

Wednesday

Thursday

Friday

Saturday

Sunday

Places to Go

People to See

Things to Do

Special Reminders

Week 35

nday

sday

dnesday

rsday

ay

rday

day

- ◯
- ◯
- ◯
- ◯
- ◯
- ◯

People to See

- ◯
- ◯
- ◯
- ◯
- ◯
- ◯

Things to Do

- ◯
- ◯
- ◯
- ◯
- ◯
- ◯
- ◯
- ◯
- ◯
- ◯
- ◯
- ◯

Special Reminders

- ◯
- ◯
- ◯
- ◯
- ◯
- ◯

Week 36

Monday

Tuesday

Wednesday

Thursday

Friday

Saturday

Sunday

Places to Go

People to See

Things to Do

Special Reminders

Week 37

nday

esday

dnesday

ursday

day

urday

nday

Places to Go

○
○
○
○
○
○

People to See

○
○
○
○
○
○

Things to Do

○
○
○
○
○
○
○
○
○
○
○
○

Special Reminders

○
○
○
○
○
○
○

Week 38

Monday

Tuesday

Wednesday

Thursday

Friday

Saturday

Sunday

Places to Go

○
○
○
○
○
○

People to See

○
○
○
○
○
○

Things to Do

○
○
○
○
○
○
○
○
○
○
○
○

Special Reminders

○
○
○
○
○
○

Week 39

nday

esday

dnesday

ursday

day

urday

nday

Week 40

Monday

Tuesday

Wednesday

Thursday

Friday

Saturday

Sunday

Places to Go

People to See

Things to Do

Special Reminders

Week 41

day

day

nesday

sday

ay

rday

day

○
○
○
○
○
○

○
○
○
○
○
○

○
○
○
○
○
○
○
○
○
○
○
○

○
○
○
○
○
○

Week 42

Monday

Tuesday

Wednesday

Thursday

Friday

Saturday

Sunday

Places to Go
-
-
-
-
-
-

People to See
-
-
-
-
-
-

Things to Do
-
-
-
-
-
-
-
-
-
-
-
-

Special Reminders
-
-
-
-
-
-

Week 43

nday

esday

ednesday

ursday

day

urday

nday

Places to Go
○
○
○
○
○
○

People to See
○
○
○
○
○
○

Things to Do
○
○
○
○
○
○
○
○
○
○
○
○

Special Reminders
○
○
○
○
○
○
○

Week 44

Monday

Tuesday

Wednesday

Thursday

Friday

Saturday

Sunday

Places to Go
- ○
- ○
- ○
- ○
- ○
- ○

People to See
- ○
- ○
- ○
- ○
- ○
- ○

Things to Do
- ○
- ○
- ○
- ○
- ○
- ○
- ○
- ○
- ○
- ○
- ○
- ○

Special Reminders
- ○
- ○
- ○
- ○
- ○
- ○

Week 45

nday

sday

dnesday

irsday

day

urday

iday

Places to Go
○
○
○
○
○
○

People to See
○
○
○
○
○
○

Things to Do
○
○
○
○
○
○
○
○
○
○
○
○

Special Reminders
○
○
○
○
○
○
○

Week 46

Monday

Tuesday

Wednesday

Thursday

Friday

Saturday

Sunday

Places to Go

People to See

Things to Do

Special Reminders

Week 47

nday

sday

lnesday

rsday

ay

rday

day

People to See

Things to Do

Special Reminders

Week 48

Monday

Tuesday

Wednesday

Thursday

Friday

Saturday

Sunday

Places to Go
- ○
- ○
- ○
- ○
- ○
- ○

People to See
- ○
- ○
- ○
- ○
- ○
- ○

Things to Do
- ○
- ○
- ○
- ○
- ○
- ○
- ○
- ○
- ○
- ○
- ○
- ○

Special Reminders
- ○
- ○
- ○
- ○
- ○
- ○

Week 49

nday

esday

ednesday

ursday

day

urday

day

Week 50

Monday

Tuesday

Wednesday

Thursday

Friday

Saturday

Sunday

Places to Go

People to See

Things to Do

Special Reminders

Week 51

nday

esday

dnesday

ursday

day

urday

day

Places to Go

○
○
○
○
○
○

People to See

○
○
○
○
○
○

Things to Do

○
○
○
○
○
○
○
○
○
○
○
○

Special Reminders

○
○
○
○
○
○

Week 52

Monday

Tuesday

Wednesday

Thursday

Friday

Saturday

Sunday

Places to Go
- ○
- ○
- ○
- ○
- ○
- ○

People to See
- ○
- ○
- ○
- ○
- ○

Things to Do
- ○
- ○
- ○
- ○
- ○
- ○
- ○
- ○
- ○
- ○
- ○

Special Reminders
- ○
- ○
- ○
- ○
- ○
- ○

Week 53

day

day

nesday

sday

ay

rday

lay

Places to Go

People to See

Things to Do

Special Reminders

My Personal Goals

This format will help you clarify your long-term goals. Be specific when listing goals, include at least 3 actions needed in order to achieve your goals, and don't forget a due date to ensure you take action. Keep this list in a place where you will see it each day; it will really help you stay focused on what's most important to you!

MY GOALS	ACTION STEPS	DUE DATE

LONG TERM

1.
2.
3.

1.
2.
3.

SHORT TERM

1.
2.
3.

1.
2.
3.

NOW

1.
2.
3.

1.
2.
3.

My Personal Goals

This format will help you clarify your long-term goals. Be specific when listing goals, include at least 3 actions needed in order to achieve your goals, and don't forget a due date to ensure you take action. Keep this list in a place where you will see it each day; it will really help you stay focused on what's most important to you!

MY GOALS	ACTION STEPS	DUE DATE
LONG TERM		
	1.	
	2.	
	3.	
	1.	
	2.	
	3.	
SHORT TERM		
	1.	
	2.	
	3.	
	1.	
	2.	
	3.	
NOW		
	1.	
	2.	
	3.	
	1.	
	2.	
	3.	

Vacation Planning

DATES:
LOCATION:
BUDGET:

GETTING THERE

CAR RENTAL

LODGING

WHAT TO PACK

RECOMMENDED SIGHTS/RESTAURANTS

ITINERARY

NOTES:

Packing List

ESSENTIALS

Tickets
Passports
Car Rental Info
Itinerary
Reservation Info
Cell Phone Charger
Car Cell Phone Charger
Foreign Currency
Wallet/Purse
Medications

CLOTHING

Undergarments/Socks
Shirts/Blouses
Jeans/Pants/Shorts
Sweaters
Dresses/Skirts
Jacket
Pajamas/Robe/Slippers
Shoes/Sneakers
Workout Clothing

TOILETRIES

Shampoo/Conditioner
Cleansers/Soap
Toothbrush/Toothpaste/Floss
Cosmetics
Deodorant
Lip Balm
Brush/Comb
Razor/Shaving Cream
Contact Lens Solution

MISCELLANEOUS

- Jewelry/Watch
- Hairdryer
- Camera/Video Camera
- Memory Cards
- Glasses/Sunglasses
- Travel Guidebooks
- Travel Journal
- Books/Magazines
- First Aid Kit
- Antibacterial Wipes/Lotion
- Stain Removal Wipes

FOR THE KIDS

- Stroller
- Diapers/Wipes/Changing
- Pad
- Diaper Bag
- Food/Formula
- Bottles
- Sippy Cups
- Utensils
- Bibs
- Medicines
- Toys/Games
- Stuffed Animal
- Blanket
- Books
- Activity Books
- Handheld Games
-
-
-
-
-

SKI ESSENTIALS

- Waterproof Ski Jacket/Pants
- Long Underwear
- Skis/Boots/Poles
- Ski Helmet
- Goggles
- Ski Gloves
- Neck Warmer
- Hat/Headband
- Ski Socks
- Hand/Foot Warmers
- Turtlenecks/Extra Sweaters
- Snow Boots
- Ski Bag

BEACH ESSENTIALS

- Swimsuit/Cover Up
- Sunscreen/After-Sun Lotion
- Beach Towels
- Beach Chairs
- Beach Umbrella
- Goggles
- Beach/Pool Toys
- Sunhat
- Sandals
- Beach Bag

OTHER

-
-
-
-
-

Websites & Passwords

WEBSITE	USERNAME	PASSWORD

Websites & Passwords

WEBSITE	USERNAME	PASSWORD

Websites & Passwords

WEBSITE	USERNAME	PASSWORD

Websites & Passwords

WEBSITE	USERNAME	PASSWORD

Notes

Notes

Notes

Notes

Notes

Notes

Notes

Party Planning

DETAILS:

MENU

BEVERAGES

GUEST NAME

RSVP Y/N

Party Planning

DETAILS:

MENU

BEVERAGES

GUEST NAME

RSVP Y/N

Party Planning

DETAILS:

MENU

BEVERAGES

GUEST NAME

RSVP Y/N

Party Planning

DETAILS:

MENU

BEVERAGES

GUEST NAME

RSVP Y/N

Christmas Day Planner

GUEST NAME	# OF ADULTS	# OF KIDS	FOOD ITEM TO BRING

TOTAL # OF GUESTS

GROCERIES

ZERS:

S:

TS:

GES:

Grocery List

FRUITS
Apples
Bananas
Oranges
Lemons
Berries
Grapes
Melons

VEGETABLES
Lettuce
Spinach
Carrots
Onions
Garlic
Tomatoes
Cucumbers
Squash
Potatoes
Broccoli

MEAT
Beef
Chicken
Turkey
Fish
Seafood
Pork
Sausage
Hot Dogs
Hamburgers
Cold Cuts

DAIRY
Milk
Juice
Cheese
Butter
Eggs
Tortillas
Yogurt
Whipped Cream

PACKAGED
Chips
Cookies
Crackers
Popcorn
Pretzels
Nuts
Candy
Dips/Salsa
Fruit Cups
Energy Bars

BREADS
White
Wheat
Fresh Baked
Bagels
Muffins
English Muffins
Pita
Rolls
Donuts/Pastries

GRAINS
Pasta
Rice
Couscous
Dried Beans
Stuffing
Bread Crumbs

BREAKFAST FOOD
Oatmeal
Pancake Mix
Granola
Cereal Bars
Syrup
Cereals

BAKING GOODS
Baking Mixes
Flours
Sugars

CANNED
Soup
Broth
Tomatoes
Pasta Sauce
Beans
Tuna
Fruits
Vegetables

BEVERAGES
Soda
Beer/Wine
Energy Drinks
Juice
Water

MISCELLANEOUS
Ketchup
Mayonnaise
Salad Dressing
Peanut Butter
Jelly
Coffee
Tea
Oils
Vinegar
Salt
Pepper
Spices

FROZEN
Ice Cream
Waffles
Pizza
Fries
Bread
Meals
Snacks
Juice
Vegetables

HOUSEHOLD GOO
Cleaning Products
Dish Liquid
Hand Soap
All-purpose
Bathroom
Floor/Carpet
Wood/Furniture
Glass/Window
Sponges
Trash Bags
Air Freshener
Hand Sanitizer
Miscellaneous

LAUNDRY
Detergent
Fabric Softener
Bleach
Starch
Stain Remover

PAPER PRODUCTS
Napkins
Paper Towels
Facial Tissue
Bathroom Tissue
Paper Plates
Paper Cups

MISC. HOUSEHOLD
Lunch Bags
Storage Bags
Storage Containers
Batteries
Coffee Filters

OTHER

Grocery List

ITS
es
nas
ges
ons
es
es
ns

ETABLES
ce
ch
ots
ns
c
toes
mbers
sh
oes
coli

T
ken
ey

od

ge
Dogs
burgers
Cuts

RY

se
r

las
t
ped Cream

PACKAGED
Chips
Cookies
Crackers
Popcorn
Pretzels
Nuts
Candy
Dips/Salsa
Fruit Cups
Energy Bars

BREADS
White
Wheat
Fresh Baked
Bagels
Muffins
English Muffins
Pita
Rolls
Donuts/Pastries

GRAINS
Pasta
Rice
Couscous
Dried Beans
Stuffing
Bread Crumbs

BREAKFAST FOOD
Oatmeal
Pancake Mix
Granola
Cereal Bars
Syrup
Cereals

BAKING GOODS
Baking Mixes
Flours
Sugars

CANNED
Soup
Broth
Tomatoes
Pasta Sauce
Beans
Tuna
Fruits
Vegetables

BEVERAGES
Soda
Beer/Wine
Energy Drinks
Juice
Water

MISCELLANEOUS
Ketchup
Mayonnaise
Salad Dressing
Peanut Butter
Jelly
Coffee
Tea
Oils
Vinegar
Salt
Pepper
Spices

FROZEN
Ice Cream
Waffles
Pizza
Fries
Bread
Meals
Snacks
Juice
Vegetables

HOUSEHOLD GOODS
Cleaning Products
Dish Liquid
Hand Soap
All-purpose
Bathroom
Floor/Carpet
Wood/Furniture
Glass/Window
Sponges
Trash Bags
Air Freshener
Hand Sanitizer
Miscellaneous

LAUNDRY
Detergent
Fabric Softener
Bleach
Starch
Stain Remover

PAPER PRODUCTS
Napkins
Paper Towels
Facial Tissue
Bathroom Tissue
Paper Plates
Paper Cups

MISC. HOUSEHOLD
Lunch Bags
Storage Bags
Storage Containers
Batteries
Coffee Filters

OTHER

Grocery List

FRUITS
Apples
Bananas
Oranges
Lemons
Berries
Grapes
Melons

VEGETABLES
Lettuce
Spinach
Carrots
Onions
Garlic
Tomatoes
Cucumbers
Squash
Potatoes
Broccoli

MEAT
Beef
Chicken
Turkey
Fish
Seafood
Pork
Sausage
Hot Dogs
Hamburgers
Cold Cuts

DAIRY
Milk
Juice
Cheese
Butter
Eggs
Tortillas
Yogurt
Whipped Cream

PACKAGED
Chips
Cookies
Crackers
Popcorn
Pretzels
Nuts
Candy
Dips/Salsa
Fruit Cups
Energy Bars

BREADS
White
Wheat
Fresh Baked
Bagels
Muffins
English Muffins
Pita
Rolls
Donuts/Pastries

GRAINS
Pasta
Rice
Couscous
Dried Beans
Stuffing
Bread Crumbs

BREAKFAST FOOD
Oatmeal
Pancake Mix
Granola
Cereal Bars
Syrup
Cereals

BAKING GOODS
Baking Mixes
Flours
Sugars

CANNED
Soup
Broth
Tomatoes
Pasta Sauce
Beans
Tuna
Fruits
Vegetables

BEVERAGES
Soda
Beer/Wine
Energy Drinks
Juice
Water

MISCELLANEOUS
Ketchup
Mayonnaise
Salad Dressing
Peanut Butter
Jelly
Coffee
Tea
Oils
Vinegar
Salt
Pepper
Spices

FROZEN
Ice Cream
Waffles
Pizza
Fries
Bread
Meals
Snacks
Juice
Vegetables

HOUSEHOLD GOO
Cleaning Products
Dish Liquid
Hand Soap
All-purpose
Bathroom
Floor/Carpet
Wood/Furniture
Glass/Window
Sponges
Trash Bags
Air Freshener
Hand Sanitizer
Miscellaneous

LAUNDRY
Detergent
Fabric Softener
Bleach
Starch
Stain Remover

PAPER PRODUCTS
Napkins
Paper Towels
Facial Tissue
Bathroom Tissue
Paper Plates
Paper Cups

MISC. HOUSEHOLD
Lunch Bags
Storage Bags
Storage Containers
Batteries
Coffee Filters

OTHER

Grocery List

JITS
les
anas
nges
10ns
ries
pes
ons

GETABLES
:uce
1ach
rots
ons
lic
1atoes
:umbers
ash
atoes
:ccoli

AT
f
:ken
key

food
k
sage
: Dogs
inburgers
d Cuts

IRY
t
e
ese
ter
s
tillas
urt
ipped Cream

PACKAGED
Chips
Cookies
Crackers
Popcorn
Pretzels
Nuts
Candy
Dips/Salsa
Fruit Cups
Energy Bars

BREADS
White
Wheat
Fresh Baked
Bagels
Muffins
English Muffins
Pita
Rolls
Donuts/Pastries

GRAINS
Pasta
Rice
Couscous
Dried Beans
Stuffing
Bread Crumbs

BREAKFAST FOOD
Oatmeal
Pancake Mix
Granola
Cereal Bars
Syrup
Cereals

BAKING GOODS
Baking Mixes
Flours
Sugars

CANNED
Soup
Broth
Tomatoes
Pasta Sauce
Beans
Tuna
Fruits
Vegetables

BEVERAGES
Soda
Beer/Wine
Energy Drinks
Juice
Water

MISCELLANEOUS
Ketchup
Mayonnaise
Salad Dressing
Peanut Butter
Jelly
Coffee
Tea
Oils
Vinegar
Salt
Pepper
Spices

FROZEN
Ice Cream
Waffles
Pizza
Fries
Bread
Meals
Snacks
Juice
Vegetables

HOUSEHOLD GOODS
Cleaning Products
Dish Liquid
Hand Soap
All-purpose
Bathroom
Floor/Carpet
Wood/Furniture
Glass/Window
Sponges
Trash Bags
Air Freshener
Hand Sanitizer
Miscellaneous

LAUNDRY
Detergent
Fabric Softener
Bleach
Starch
Stain Remover

PAPER PRODUCTS
Napkins
Paper Towels
Facial Tissue
Bathroom Tissue
Paper Plates
Paper Cups

MISC. HOUSEHOLD
Lunch Bags
Storage Bags
Storage Containers
Batteries
Coffee Filters

OTHER

2020

January
```
Su Mo Tu We Th Fr Sa
         1  2  3  4
 5  6  7  8  9 10 11
12 13 14 15 16 17 18
19 20 21 22 23 24 25
26 27 28 29 30 31
2○ 10○ 17○ 24●
```

February
```
Su Mo Tu We Th Fr Sa
                  1
 2  3  4  5  6  7  8
 9 10 11 12 13 14 15
16 17 18 19 20 21 22
23 24 25 26 27 28 29
1○ 9○ 15○ 23●
```

March
```
Su Mo Tu We Th Fr Sa
 1  2  3  4  5  6  7
 8  9 10 11 12 13 14
15 16 17 18 19 20 21
22 23 24 25 26 27 28
29 30 31
2○ 9○ 16○ 24●
```

April
```
Su Mo Tu We Th Fr Sa
          1  2  3  4
 5  6  7  8  9 10 11
12 13 14 15 16 17 18
19 20 21 22 23 24 25
26 27 28 29 30
1○ 7○ 14○ 22● 30○
```

May
```
Su Mo Tu We Th Fr Sa
                1  2
 3  4  5  6  7  8  9
10 11 12 13 14 15 16
17 18 19 20 21 22 23
24 25 26 27 28 29 30
31
7○ 14○ 22● 29○
```

June
```
Su Mo Tu We Th Fr Sa
    1  2  3  4  5  6
 7  8  9 10 11 12 13
14 15 16 17 18 19 20
21 22 23 24 25 26 27
28 29 30
5○ 13○ 21● 28○
```

July
```
Su Mo Tu We Th Fr Sa
          1  2  3  4
 5  6  7  8  9 10 11
12 13 14 15 16 17 18
19 20 21 22 23 24 25
26 27 28 29 30 31
5○ 12○ 20● 27○
```

August
```
Su Mo Tu We Th Fr Sa
                   1
 2  3  4  5  6  7  8
 9 10 11 12 13 14 15
16 17 18 19 20 21 22
23 24 25 26 27 28 29
30 31
3○ 11○ 18● 25○
```

September
```
Su Mo Tu We Th Fr Sa
       1  2  3  4  5
 6  7  8  9 10 11 12
13 14 15 16 17 18 19
20 21 22 23 24 25 26
27 28 29 30
2○ 10○ 17● 23○
```

October
```
Su Mo Tu We Th Fr Sa
             1  2  3
 4  5  6  7  8  9 10
11 12 13 14 15 16 17
18 19 20 21 22 23 24
25 26 27 28 29 30 31
1○ 9○ 16● 23○ 31○
```

November
```
Su Mo Tu We Th Fr Sa
 1  2  3  4  5  6  7
 8  9 10 11 12 13 14
15 16 17 18 19 20 21
22 23 24 25 26 27 28
29 30
8○ 15● 21○ 30○
```

December
```
Su Mo Tu We Th Fr Sa
       1  2  3  4  5
 6  7  8  9 10 11 12
13 14 15 16 17 18 19
20 21 22 23 24 25 26
27 28 29 30 31
7○ 14● 21○ 29○
```

2021

January
```
Su Mo Tu We Th Fr Sa
                1  2
 3  4  5  6  7  8  9
10 11 12 13 14 15 16
17 18 19 20 21 22 23
24 25 26 27 28 29 30
31
6○ 13○ 20○ 28○
```

February
```
Su Mo Tu We Th Fr Sa
    1  2  3  4  5  6
 7  8  9 10 11 12 13
14 15 16 17 18 19 20
21 22 23 24 25 26 27
28
4○ 11○ 19○ 27○
```

March
```
Su Mo Tu We Th Fr Sa
    1  2  3  4  5  6
 7  8  9 10 11 12 13
14 15 16 17 18 19 20
21 22 23 24 25 26 27
28 29 30 31
5○ 13○ 21○ 28○
```

April
```
Su Mo Tu We Th Fr Sa
             1  2  3
 4  5  6  7  8  9 10
11 12 13 14 15 16 17
18 19 20 21 22 23 24
25 26 27 28 29 30
4○ 11○ 20○ 26○
```

May
```
Su Mo Tu We Th Fr Sa
                   1
 2  3  4  5  6  7  8
 9 10 11 12 13 14 15
16 17 18 19 20 21 22
23 24 25 26 27 28 29
30 31
3○ 11○ 19○ 26○
```

June
```
Su Mo Tu We Th Fr Sa
       1  2  3  4  5
 6  7  8  9 10 11 12
13 14 15 16 17 18 19
20 21 22 23 24 25 26
27 28 29 30
2○ 10○ 17○ 24○
```

July
```
Su Mo Tu We Th Fr Sa
             1  2  3
 4  5  6  7  8  9 10
11 12 13 14 15 16 17
18 19 20 21 22 23 24
25 26 27 28 29 30 31
1○ 9○ 17○ 23○ 31○
```

August
```
Su Mo Tu We Th Fr Sa
 1  2  3  4  5  6  7
 8  9 10 11 12 13 14
15 16 17 18 19 20 21
22 23 24 25 26 27 28
29 30 31
8○ 15○ 22○ 30○
```

September
```
Su Mo Tu We Th Fr Sa
          1  2  3  4
 5  6  7  8  9 10 11
12 13 14 15 16 17 18
19 20 21 22 23 24 25
26 27 28 29 30
6○ 13○ 20○ 26○
```

October
```
Su Mo Tu We Th Fr Sa
                1  2
 3  4  5  6  7  8  9
10 11 12 13 14 15 16
17 18 19 20 21 22 23
24 25 26 27 28 29 30
31
6○ 12○ 20○ 28○
```

November
```
Su Mo Tu We Th Fr Sa
    1  2  3  4  5  6
 7  8  9 10 11 12 13
14 15 16 17 18 19 20
21 22 23 24 25 26 27
28 29 30
4○ 11○ 19○ 27○
```

December
```
Su Mo Tu We Th Fr Sa
             1  2
 5  6  7  8  9 10 11
12 13 14 15 16
19 20 21 22 23
26 27 28 29 30
4○ 10○ 18○ 26○
```

2022

January
```
Su Mo Tu We Th Fr Sa
                   1
 2  3  4  5  6  7  8
 9 10 11 12 13 14 15
16 17 18 19 20 21 22
23 24 25 26 27 28 29
30 31
2● 9○ 17○ 25○
```

February
```
Su Mo Tu We Th Fr Sa
       1  2  3  4  5
 6  7  8  9 10 11 12
13 14 15 16 17 18 19
20 21 22 23 24 25 26
27 28
1● 8○ 16○ 23○
```

March
```
Su Mo Tu We Th Fr Sa
       1  2  3  4  5
 6  7  8  9 10 11 12
13 14 15 16 17 18 19
20 21 22 23 24 25 26
27 28 29 30 31
2● 10○ 18○ 25○
```

April
```
Su Mo Tu We Th Fr Sa
                1  2
 3  4  5  6  7  8  9
10 11 12 13 14 15 16
17 18 19 20 21 22 23
24 25 26 27 28 29 30
1○ 9○ 16○ 23○ 30●
```

May
```
Su Mo Tu We Th Fr Sa
 1  2  3  4  5  6  7
 8  9 10 11 12 13 14
15 16 17 18 19 20 21
22 23 24 25 26 27 28
29 30 31
8○ 16○ 22○ 30●
```

June
```
Su Mo Tu We Th Fr Sa
          1  2  3  4
 5  6  7  8  9 10 11
12 13 14 15 16 17 18
19 20 21 22 23 24 25
26 27 28 29 30
7○ 14○ 20○ 28●
```

July
```
Su Mo Tu We Th Fr Sa
                1  2
 3  4  5  6  7  8  9
10 11 12 13 14 15 16
17 18 19 20 21 22 23
24 25 26 27 28 29 30
31
6○ 13○ 20○ 28●
```

August
```
Su Mo Tu We Th Fr Sa
    1  2  3  4  5  6
 7  8  9 10 11 12 13
14 15 16 17 18 19 20
21 22 23 24 25 26 27
28 29 30 31
5○ 11○ 19○ 27●
```

September
```
Su Mo Tu We Th Fr Sa
             1  2  3
 4  5  6  7  8  9 10
11 12 13 14 15 16 17
18 19 20 21 22 23 24
25 26 27 28 29 30
3○ 10○ 17○ 25●
```

October
```
Su Mo Tu We Th Fr Sa
                1
 2  3  4  5  6  7  8
 9 10 11 12 13 14 15
16 17 18 19 20 21 22
23 24 25 26 27 28 29
30 31
2○ 9○ 17○ 25●
```

November
```
Su Mo Tu We Th Fr Sa
       1  2  3  4  5
 6  7  8  9 10 11 12
13 14 15 16 17 18 19
20 21 22 23 24 25 26
27 28 29 30
1○ 8○ 16○ 23● 30○
```

December
```
Su Mo Tu We Th Fr Sa
             1  2  3
 4  5  6  7  8  9 10
11 12 13 14 15 16 17
18 19 20 21 22 23 24
25 26 27 28 29 30 31
7○ 16○ 23● 29○
```

2023

January
```
Su Mo Tu We Th Fr Sa
 1  2  3  4  5  6  7
 8  9 10 11 12 13 14
15 16 17 18 19 20 21
22 23 24 25 26 27 28
29 30 31
6○ 14○ 21● 28○
```

February
```
Su Mo Tu We Th Fr Sa
          1  2  3  4
 5  6  7  8  9 10 11
12 13 14 15 16 17 18
19 20 21 22 23 24 25
26 27 28
5○ 13○ 20● 27○
```

March
```
Su Mo Tu We Th Fr Sa
             1  2  3
 5  6  7  8  9 10 11
12 13 14 15 16 17
19 20 21 22 23
26 27 28 29 30
7○ 14○ 21● 28○
```

April
```
Su Mo Tu We Th Fr Sa
                   1
 2  3  4  5  6  7  8
 9 10 11 12 13 14 15
16 17 18 19 20 21 22
23 24 25 26 27 28 29
30
6○ 13○ 20● 27○
```

May
```
Su Mo Tu We Th Fr Sa
    1  2  3  4  5  6
 7  8  9 10 11 12 13
14 15 16 17 18 19 20
21 22 23 24 25 26 27
28 29 30 31
5○ 12○ 19● 27○
```

June
```
Su Mo Tu We Th Fr Sa
                1  2
 4  5  6  7  8  9
11 12 13 14 15 16
18 19 20 21 22
25 26 27 28 29 30
3○ 10○ 18● 26○
```

July
```
Su Mo Tu We Th Fr Sa
                   1
 2  3  4  5  6  7  8
 9 10 11 12 13 14 15
16 17 18 19 20 21 22
23 24 25 26 27 28 29
30 31
3○ 9○ 17○ 25○
```

August
```
Su Mo Tu We Th Fr Sa
       1  2  3  4  5
 6  7  8  9 10 11 12
13 14 15 16 17 18 19
20 21 22 23 24 25 26
27 28 29 30 31
1○ 8○ 16○ 24○ 30○
```

September
```
Su Mo Tu We Th Fr
             1
 3  4  5  6  7
10 11 12 13 14 1
17 18 19 20 21
24 25 26 27 28 2
6○ 14○ 22○ 29
```

October
```
Su Mo Tu We Th Fr Sa
 1  2  3  4  5  6  7
 8  9 10 11 12 13 14
15 16 17 18 19 20 21
22 23 24 25 26 27 28
29 30 31
6○ 14● 21○ 28○
```

November
```
Su Mo Tu We Th Fr Sa
          1  2  3  4
 5  6  7  8  9 10 11
12 13 14 15 16 17 18
19 20 21 22 23 24 25
26 27 28 29 30
5○ 13● 20○ 27○
```

December
```
Su Mo Tu We Th Fr
             1
 3  4  5  6  7  8
10 11 12 13 14 1
17 18 19 20 21 2
24 25 26 27 28 2
31
5○ 12● 19○ 2
```

Printed in Great Britain
by Amazon

77603983R00068